A Taste
Of Light

Jo Nelson

Acknowledgments

The following poems have been published:
La Push in **Art Access**
Whitewash and Vie en Rose in **the Cool Traveler**
Baltimore 1968 and Clickety Clack in **Main Street Rag**
In Heidelberg and In Zurich in **the Montserat Review**
Riding the Rag and Bolden in **Pig Iron**
Road Warrior in **Pleiades**
Tongues in **Psychic Pathways**
Triggers and Schrei in **the San Fernando Poetry
    Journal**
Eating Up the Road and Mordida in **the Seattle Five
    Plus One: Poetry**

First Edition.

A TASTE OF LIGHT
Copyright © 2000   Jo Nelson

Cover image
Copyright © 2000   Stephen Quiller

yeolde@webcom.com - www.yeolde.org

ISBN: 1-889289-48-5

Printed in the United States by
Morris Publishing
3212 East Highway 30
Kearney, NE 68847
1-800-650-7888

To my mother who taught me to look for the wonder, my father who taught me to hear the music, and my brother Michael who believed in me before I believed in myself.

TABLE OF CONTENTS

Promised Land

Das Firmament blaut ewig und die Erde

Wird lange fest steh'n und aufblühn im Lenz.
Du, aber, Mensch, we lang lebst denn du?
Night hundert Jahre darfst du dich ergötzen
An all dem morschen Tande dieser Erde!
                                   —Mahler, Das Lied von der Erde

The firmament blues forever and the earth

will long remain fast and blossom in spring.
But you, mortal one, how long will you live then?
No hundred years will you amuse yourself
with all the fleeting pleasures of this earth.
                                   (translation, the author)

1

Eating Up the Road

The Second world War force-fed America
with the cadence of the road -
fifty Chevys, big bumpered, hunkered down,
their fins and tails flailed
paths of black topped winding
DesotoFord grills grinning silver toothed
Crosleys and Henry J's made
forty five miles to the gallon
with gas so plentiful, no one noticed
boys fresh off the farm
drank their cafe au lait, their vin ordinair
slouched toward Hollywood
pasteboard washed white homes -
all around those picket fences
love and drugs painted colors
film makers infected
the innocent way we saved
perfumed sex and rampant consumption
played full houses banks drafted
people to spend all their time
chasing dreams down the rolling endless
prairies and grain fields;
rivers muddy with cows
lined up the roads black and white
striped country towns
drowned in factory chic
when we bombed engines to overdrive
moving vans cruising the national
debt grew in proportion to automated
eating up the roadsides -
Boston Commons, the Loop, Saint Louis
arched the golden bay at San Francisco
aquariums flooded with angels
while the Valley grew poppies
and peach skin bikinis on rooftops
waited for the surf to rise.

Repris

Catch a Reymus fizz at Cliff House.
Bloody Marys crowd the Brando walls
while out the windows,
waves break over seal rocks
and tingle back the bar
of sunlight over leather chairs,
the days when San Francisco
trolleys belled
and fishermen silvered the wharf
with webbed scales
sails drowned in wind
and the Presidio bluffed
the golden gate white
Russian Hill captains built -
the winding azure
glass stained gut red
as the fireball drowning.

Paper Chase

Hollywood died a few years back
and no one knew it
because the speed of light
refracts the sender
and the beat that replaced
hymns to dying gods
were not so easily spent
as the surrogate violence;
the ersatz bloodtears
in a million living room
eyes glued to the autonomic
shutter stop of the trivial
wet dreams of wealth unrequited
or madonaslut love
of the dragons St. Porsche chases
through downtowns rising
above the stoned streets and sewers
too lethal to breathe the night air.
The talking shadows bemuse
the fast forward fugues, the pickets
burning the San Andreas.

Ghost Town

This is the lonesome town
you passed through on the train
and thanked the gods
you didn't have to stay.
Stairways into dark escape the pavement
striped and numbered bare;
windows stare through signs
of last years' sales.
People came from anywhere,
the small town touch -
now their hollow footsteps strut
streets that go nowhere -
headlights only brush
the ghosts down.

Jabberwok

Talk shows hum midnight to dawn
ways coffee stained
Formica tables blending diners in neon
cups thick as day-old
bread spreads to jam up the register;
quarters and dimes
sing duos, country blues,
thigh sighing gear shifts clutch
the down time windows whistle;
poles flash the meaning of wood
through stone tunnels and glass-eyed
horses on tired asphalt
scream the miles measured
when stars dim headlong rush
of voices voices voices.

Portland

Hills embrace Victorian ladies,
lace the walks with rose attar -
a century in each petal nuance dried in pot pourri.
Roots shake rain to ground;
spout fountains 'round carved friezes,
spindles turned from trees.
Steel spins rivers and air;
sirens string webs of sound through the turns
of fortune old store buildings trace -
green grocer, fish monger, tailor -
faded in the rise of glass.
Galleries link arms under elms
where leaves whisper the cobbles
and crows stare the filtered highlights
of sidewalk lattes
mingled with books and dust.
The screes of gulls drown the waterfront;
scumble past posh shops and hostels,
their gaunt shadows softened with pastel.
The Willamette and Columbia
roll sailboats, tankers, tugs and trawlers;
red cranes load   unload
a jazz sea chantey
that strafes the rocking hulls; traces
the seaward slide of trade through steel lace.

Dawned

Docks slip from morning slumber
before fog awakes
day's gray tongue -
gulls shrill the metered calm
and water draws the luffing sails
through slap of wood and line;
through the fine gradations
espresso bleeds from
the shine on rough wood.
A cough; a muffled step amends
the flow of calm -
nets and ropes coil a motor roar;
the creaking lift of sail
hungers for sun's touch,
the flop of open swell
that edge us into dawn.

La Push

Floating dragons whisper winds,
sunsets stalk the random moons
that float a shadowed sky;
mystic breath teems silent teardrops;
salt spray scrapes the shells on rock.
Spirits waver, wander free
about the sounding driftwood.
Time locked mist obscures the now
until you feel the primal rush
of wind-torn waves and sheltered dunes.
Beyond the looking glass of sand,
a flash of white horizon,
jade cascading tongues of foam.
Moon mirrors ghost advance.
Tides rush a weathered stone,
a feather fleur-de lis etched white
against the darkling sand reflection —
bones of new dreams.

Night Shift at the Navy Yard

Rain bathes the tear sweat
of life bleak as car swarms
waiting for the ferry
to pinpoint lights incandescing
the black river tunnels
we run.
Gray shapes hunker
down rain washed concrete;
the fly blow parking lots
staring empty as school yard
doorways gaping Saturday free
and roofs swaying the weight
of neglect.
Oil clogs waterspore; spongesoil lament
taints dumping the council ignores
for the ships bring money
to a town empty as tin cans.

Ferries Crossing

The firefly skyline
glides from dark the water keeps.
We feed the fishes wind,
the whoosh of steel;
the turning grime of engines.
Below, waves
coat the black with light licked foam;
hills stretch into mountains
of sound piers float along.
Sky shards grow -
awe struck,
we walk the open maw.

Pioneer Squared

Shadows walk the long city dark.
Pigeons feather white scratching for dirt
the trees gobble like cocks.
Bricks window blank Occidental Avenue
after five o'clock hushes the pulse
to leave the bronze bull quiet
between the swish of cars or ferry docking.
Light flashes neon shaded granite —
wild rock clouds pass invisible as stars
hang light years over totems poled.
Benches lean on their ears,
breathe in rhythm voices break hostile.
Starlings settle coats shed for night's yawning beds
but downtown struggles to maintain
condos and bars blazing a sun swallow needle.
Elliott Bay spells walls of words
caught wingless in spindrift.
Moonsilvered tables dot
heavy metals spilled from the bars.

Fanfare for the Common

Steel Prime

Crab claws click the brick sidewalks doorways swallow
cadres of head bands dripping salt venom
assault weapon caches
pray for the right to kill anything out of Kevlar,
kill in the name of the video
the body count mounts;
father tongues glue dreams of tight butt muscle gridirons
that pin stripe plastic vaults.

Market

Blue deep, the Sound and mountains steep
the music mirror swells gull storms
that fuse clam and bell, fuse ferry to sun and sting sails
to crack the rain shell wide enough
for the sky to purge horse carts
and trolleys bell hulls that slice the Sound.
Voices and face shapes harry the blacktop -
dragons, elephants; dog joggers lapping
kites hawk lazy balloons filled with flesh silver scaled
and sweet musky scent of papaya.
Sun glistens apple skins red as faces soak up the sun.
Heat sheens backs bent under the white hot torch;
spray bottles freckle spinach and chicory buttercrunch.
Awnings ring ice cream and snow cones;
wind socks unleash foam banner stalls where pea pods prod
melons
and cukes score Beefsteak tomatoes.

Harbor

Heat strobes the wheat waterfall
into steel hulls
clang the orange crane arms
that swing many tongued boxcars
over the fog soup water.
Forklifts shift the midnight winds down
black coffee eyes and talk shows lament
boxes broken to pilfer wind.

Monuments

First Avenue staggers from the weight of cranes
swinging craters empty
wine cheap apartments too close to the fall
of SAM's soundless hammer. The homeless
shift silent in the afterbirth of cuts
that leave children aimless.
The flag wind licks canyons of battered
bricks do not staunch the red flowers.

Bleed

Spit red, they splatter —
worm tongues tingle their sticky earth sweat.
Wounds ward the sucked air,
lips suck the eye stare,
white crosses the devil marks
noses and foreheads   the white pain
pans a blood rush
feathers tear from pin weeds breeding dark
swallows eye white;
swallows tongue hollowed bones
bead empty echoed on masks of flesh.

14

Cracks

Metal ratchets cracked concrete foot whisper cough;
tuberous tires telegraph glass sky grates
to city cisterns where the shades of Skid Road glide
the cobble shiny.
Black plastic spells hate and brass horses
gnash steel green jaws -
a shoe with no toe, a sock in a shell;
one crow feather fans the leftover smoke
an old one shares with blank benches
below the totem pole   pigeons polish pearl gray.
Dark rays empty window sockets;
traffic swishes gray to black
old men pass bottle sacks
before galleries of empty canvas   firewater fades;
starlings scold a carpet store always going out of business.
Sirens scrape the empty building faces,
the square stone butterfly frozen en pointes.

Garden

Zong Cha bundles flowers;
sweet, rainbow flowers —
statice, sweet peas, baby's breath.
His lips smile, his eyes hold rain
for the sweet rainbow warrior
rootless in the black chasm he swallowed.

Take-out

Sunday sermons simmer rainbow remote;
coral snakes writhe Jacob's
stained glass cathedral,
organs blasting full stop deliverance.

Resurrection

Nails tear at the skin and the skin blossoms red
as nails drive deep in his hands
splayed for the tearing nails;
spikes spit sinews of muscle bound wood
he climbs with his hands
to blood the ground shower.
Hands white as bone beads
on stone   strafe their thin light
worn marble flesh;
an Angellus of bullets
thumpscream the living dead
tongue bells overlay to cross themselves
in blue pain thunder.

Mission

hot soup showers and pallets tick the rain beat
of hymns and steel folding chair strings -
but it beats soggy sidewalks and dumpster tacos
between the blue POP whine
and cock crow line-up at the Millionaire Club.

Central

Sun faded Victorians see beyond downtown highlight
cherry blossom central.
Cloud eyes lace porch rail baskets flaming
cascaded lobelia.
Lawns breathe velvet buckled sidewalks,
fences spike lilac and hydrangea;
chestnuts wave high rising breezes
where ghosts walk their shadow play down
to the player piano.
Bluebirds bathe heavy wet in a rush of goldfish.
Hose mist kisses tomato beds warm from sun against cement
siren hot roses thorn
children playing baseball to a boom box ump.

Breath

Feet rat-a-tat the running path.
Lycra licks gym gyred waves of Walkmen
around Greenlake, America
where sailboards slash the sun splashed clouds
and dogs leash rollerblades.

Gap

Poppies forget their pupleyellowred.
Ducks glide the canal kayaks cut without noise;
sailboats slide under the bridge;
a tall spar cracks the daylight to choke five o'clock
rush from University to Eastlake
where downtown spires simmer Lake Union's Moat.

Wave

At Shillshole, sailboats sleep chrysalis tight.
Their naked masts stay the water burnished shield
until wind fills sail slap.
In the strait, tide runs a heady chop;
white corks bob.
Seiners crawl to dock by the Boston Whaler
in the wake of yachts;
a trawler hauls its scale flash light;
gulls dreaming dive the steelgleam;
moss bubbles trail the dark wash.

Locked

Heat hives the I-5 bass tweeter crawl;
glass wombs wall tinsel tunnels
crossed at the anger apex;
white snakes, red and blue ball
plastic yielding heat haze abutments
time stripe yellow barrels four lanes to two
gears grind puddled oil.

Phoenix

Seed stars spark the great dark howl;
heavy hang the diamond echoes;
black holes spill sibilants into the scratch of night mice
that fade before the gray ghosted owl.
Glass sculls stoned cirrus;
sun shards spike the still birthed dew.
Heat hazes green grass oases
that rise from dry wells of concrete.

Fire

White dwarfs blaze sky's navy blanket,
wear away Orion's scabbard and Ursa's bucket
open closes the margin cars park.

July wraps warm fingered, breathing diamond light -
sparks hang hard edged dreams
steam the sky spring to tether wind's territorial
tongue blades slashing the dark cat fall.
Light pangs the pain core;
seeded coats candle new waves
that lick novas from the roaring auroras.

Pink fountains red dwarfs;
tangerine sprays green vine trumpets
that hiss the blaze white —
a canned band plays Something Beautiful —
and the people   ahhh.

Moving On

I knew I had already left the city
when the wind chimes next door began to sound
cow bells on the high range a river flowed
beyond the rows of rock-hued condos,
the tangle of blackberry vine encroachments,
lawns no one mowed.
You awaken in another's dream;
you know what drawers hold knives,
where towels hide by the shower
and the mirrors by which you measure
your Doppelganger share morning naked
as you stare at the skin you shed,
cling to the fruit flies
jarring the clean lines of shelves
peach suns fill in winter cloud
and you know this year,
the answers   aren't that simple.

Road Warrior

Headlights stab each dark turn
we wind through Arizona midnight.
White crosses slash our retinas,
ghosts at odds with black and blacktop
cry behind their bones.
Heat mirages wash the roads out
white strips whisper
gray yard after graveyard curves
twisted aftermath of metal
through the hollow core
beyond our eyeballs
that blink and bind and close.
Adrenaline wrenches the wheel
gravel rattles a tire -
we stare into the threshold of crosses,
pull over and walk
until the molten engine ticks to quiet
the blaze of stars.
The red light of Betelgeuse fades
the hiss of tumbleweeds.

Away

Shoulders hunched over

        the headlight's swath

she sews stitches

        of blacktop stripes

the motor hums
from dart to seam

        sunrise pulls itself
        from desert dreams

clips each thread as
though an end means
not another start

        life pours from
        Chico and saguaro
        shadows disburse the dust

still, she pulls another
silken fabric

        pink and purple swirls
        spin their wheels

all the way to Tucson

Pastores

Ghost chords build up over Tres Piedras,
stampede through the gnarled piñones
and throw themselves at lightning's ziggurat.
Sweat and ozone, pitch and horse shit
stir bauxite veils through the dust.
Moon blue, the sky door halos pines etched black.

A raw bawling wind whips pale faced cows;
iron steamed calves scream
in the milling melange of men and hoof moos.
The hills mushroom white,
re-fuel the old cow/sheep fight owners juggle for BLM
land Spain entrusted before the westward trails won.

Here sheep belong, the Basque grasscape,
the high sombreros and coats wool lined.
Anda, anda, perros, sing the herders
todo el santo dia
and the cattlemen's necks rust red.

The road lip sidewinds from the antelope fence
to San Anton Mountain's TV relay
Spanish is the tongue crows speak
under the stone Trinity
between Tierra Amarilla and Taos.

Take Off

Rain wet, the tarmac crazy quilts city lights
dark curtain halogen halos black.
The whole hull drones propeller throb;
the sleek silver bullet
thunder scumbles flash fire -
we rise above wing tumble wind rush
our lives suspend.
Belts bend
earth bauble moon bubbled thrust.
Land maps itself in dark blanks and thin silver chains
clouds phosphoresce.
Laptop figures blur rain washed wings.
City lights trace stars our running lights rub out
and the steel casing swallows us.
Smiles deflect cramped calves.
Through the scrape of plastic forks and coffee carts,
we time the tedium.
At last, engines change.
Window banks pinpoint an Interstate;
street lights awaken fog.
A studded arrow raises like an arm for a hawk
and we dive, screaming.

Colorado Springs

The city soul is not the airport sterile
floors and windows nowhere jet rush -
it is the city buses men and women
daily working home to cook and clean
houses molding in the sun gray
auto parts and Realtor churches; breakfast diners
chrome stools perched close
and the boss greets each regular
hotcake hashbrown gravy;
acid coffee glows
Coke magnets, jalopy calendar
daze of everyyear the faces
paled by Cheyenne Mountain
digest breakfast news.
Vacant lots weed broken grass rocks
tune Chinese cheeseburgs, blackeye ribs;
the coffee acid drips
the traffic start and stop
lights Nevada Avenue Victorians
poppy lobelia gold rush proud.

Triggers

Sixteen miles northwest of the
Gateway to the Rockies,
plutonium simmered in soil
until cattle mutated from the ground water.
Cancer endemic was ignored because
the National Interest dictated it.
After all, they were only making
TRIGGERS there, weren't they?
Triggers for nuclear bombs being
what they are,
but no one talked about that.
In ventilation ducts, plutonium gas
gathered potentially more explosive
than protests outside the Flats
and still Denver slumbered,
unable to give up all those jobs
in light of economic downturns
and a few measly twisted cows.

Rescue Mission

Chopper blades pound the heavy air
as wind gusts tear away
the WHOP WHOP enough to
hear the fury of their force.
Ninety miles an hour gusts
crackles tin-laced radio voice
AND COUNTING, I think,
GOING ONCE, GOING TWICE -
I taste copper bile of life too sweet
jet rotors scream into the storm's teeth
snow level falls to ten thousand feet.
Tree tops, angry rocks
coming closer with another gust
that throws us, toy-like,
a hundred feet down.
WHOP WHOP strain of heart beat
WHOP WHOP of motor ever deeper under siege.
Boulder Canyon funnels wind death
from the Rockies
like cyclotrons ready to implode.

Dream Wake

Before the conscious decision to leave Denver,
the dream came.
I still remember the country, the hill
overlooking the Russian River,
the wildflowers grazed by salt sweat;
the house wrinkled and weathered as trees,
the odd assortment of rooms,
old fashioned plank floors
against tongue and grooved ceiling,
bricks holding a clawless tub,
closets too narrow for shoes;
casement windows looking out
to a barn with vagrant eyes.
I still remember the hexagram
of buildings and land
that dreamed me through cities dazed in glass,
through life too complex to breathe
and deposited me here.

Moving On

Finstre, schwarze Riesenfalter
Töteten der Sonne Glanz.
Ein geschlossnes Zauberbuch,
Ruht der Horizont - verschwiegen.

—Schoenberg, Pierrot Lunaire, II.8

Sinister, dark giant butterflies
killed the sun's gloss.
A closed book of incantations
calms the horizon - silent.

(translation, the author)

Clickety Clack

Tears drip against the window
outside   in -
rails articulate my bones,
heart valves open close
against reluctant dreams I leave
the click of steel on miles,
the pulse of heated blood now cold.
We climb   the mountains pass.
The cities all wear cloaks of gray,
gray sprawls warehouse malls,
crumbling, aged plants;
towns fuzz into country too much farmed
to see the templates sown
with green and brown.
Steel rails trail another gloaming,
light flickers   brush unrelenting
the sway and spin of dark.

Doppler Effects

Steel rails trail the DNA
of small towns no longer bound
to the pulse of diesel -
owls hoot the throbbing night dreams
of horses who race the wind.
Stations hover edges of smiles
benches bend in the wailing drum
of earth's ripe sweat.
Light snakes shine the spin
towns pass in the clattering sway backed;
sway back to the memories
when radio crackled the linking
news reels in movie houses
foreign wars flickered through popcorn
magic of ten cent features
that lost us in pickets
shed for something half said
in the clicking reels of smoke and light
framed to smooth the snake.

Baltimore, 1968

The ceiling peeled overhead,
lines radiated shadow dreams gone mad
as I lay at night on the bed
and listened to the lead pipes
when Yashiko or Tatjana turned on a tap.
Walls crackled platoons of roaches
the landlord sprayed after you left
a dozen messages on his answer machine
but they migrated up or down
until their systems adapted to poison.

I loved that old house turned tenement
on Old York Road.
The yard was large; oaks brushed
third story gables with shadow lace
and a magnolia petaled the grass at night
so the moon double reflected it.

This was my first apartment, my first trip East,
my first teaching job
and I filled my life with finds from the Echo Shop
and Charles Street cast-offs
before oak came back in vogue
and people braved the streets
where you watched your car through dusty windows
so no one stole the tires.

It never occurred to me scavenging was dangerous;
I was a small-town girl who could care for herself
and never had to prove it.
I roamed the blocks of row houses,
the museum and library at Hopkins,
the waterfront shops that still catered
to fishermen, longshoremen, and whores
and ate crab cakes and crab legs
boiled in barrels on the sands of the Chesapeake.
32

Our neighborhood was an anachronism -
faded Victorians clipped lawns
the high rise developers hadn't spotted;
parasol ladies cut roses from brick courtyards
and once a week, the cobbled streets
rang with hooves as old Leo sold produce
from a wooden wagon his father's father had.

A mile from the Beltway,
crickets and frogs overrode traffic.
Farms tucked among overgrowth
and barns sagged like sway backed nags
that swatted at the heat and flies
steamed the city from Memorial to Labor Day.

Line Drawing

See Chicago through the stockyard railways, cafes
with their inch-thick steaks. Men and animals ground up like
        sausages
at the edge of the nation's granary. Corn gold simmers cribs
numb cattle bawl, mill their few feet of soil.
"Hup, hup," auctioneers call the price war waged against future
stakes driven into the Heartland.

Harvester and John Deere caps block the dust their fathers
        plowed
in straight lines, blood lines, lines of boys who felt the tractor
        pull
through the roar of packing plants and offal,
through the clank of steel rails that radiate from this energy hub
like shaved herds of buffalo.

The Ell snake rattles faded neighborhoods
trading brick for stone.
Steel and glass loop Lake Michigan's Gold Coast;
the parks breathless in fat leafed Indian autumn.

The Art Institute draws a tree brush scumble,
a mariachi mambo bones roll on ivory.
Shorts and jeans, kaftans and saris,
flip-flop, sandal boot moccasin walking.
Sax sweet, rhythms pack the street theater
in a round robin drama headed for Off Broadway.

Bridges

Like cranes the buildings
strut along mud flats
unaware the watered distance
heaves to turn the tide.

Gulls scout sanded imperfections,
knowing where the clams have gone,
smarter than the piers
that bridge the now to nowhere
with half their pilings down.

Manhattan High

A clockwork grays this lightscape rises with the hum
tire trolley footvolleyhammer.
Light falls through basement windows   hard as crows
hard as their swallow beaks
marked by dust's twilight timbre.
Ten steps below the rush of soles on sidewalk,
concrete hollows metates worn down
by the everyday grinding, by the candle chimeras climb.

Velvet soft the rough rumble of the subway
updrafts crystal shadows in a feather scream.
Holes hold dark shafts so the sky can breathe,
blossom O'Keefe tableaux
too far away to see chicken roast pasta,
an apple orange arrangement in a china bowl;
violets, geraniums, a crucifix; rose red hearts.

Hackneys clop the shadow ways of Central Park —
joggers bikers rollerbladers; suits and Nikes
oranges spill spit slick sidewalks
street guitars pick for marks.

Two men slump in a Sloan diner washed in green neon;
one with apple pie coffee, one with the bluelight soup
a wrinkled waitress ladles
as she pours midnight from a steel pot.

All night, the lights flash,
all night taxis slow rain bowed headlights' pass.
Broadway reflects glass eye sidewalks -
doctors, lawyers, actors rush for cheesecake
between late shows and the Times' reviews.

No glitter in night's diamond windows
but in the garment district, clothes racks ripple;
brokers catch Asian markets
fish mongers scale in a hail of ice.
Want ads skitter from East River garbage scows.
Plastic bags hunker lumpy fat   dented cans
dump trucks bang at four a.m.
elbow the drone of yellow beaked cabs.
Roof tops waver in dawn's onslaught.

Riding the Rag

Pierre Lunaire black fall water drops
street gutter rippled -
where do they go, these old grace notes?
OH, we led the life then,
blue bones in voices moon braised
white shining worm eyes
chest smoke winding
juice squeezed eyelash rubies
crow tails dipped in earth soul;
light licked edges burned
fingers slow tongued
arms winding sweat metaphor,
swamp cooler fan fumble,
rain rumble no air.

Fifty Ferlinghetti Cats

played with the hard steel
of Henry's balustrade -
back and forth the slow parade
of paws and tails,
the hoarse Piaf meows,
the twang of six steel strings
fingered fast and loose.
Full moon shined its spot
along the sides
of Henry's old Victorian;
lighted her cracks and imperfections,
but from the way those cats sang,
you would have thought
they were jazzing Bourbon Street
with Thunderbird.

The Spirit of New Orleans

Henry played piano
to keep his soul alive at night.
He worked by day in the Vieux Carre
between the bricks and mud.
A falling wall cut short
his bass crescendos
but Henry didn't wail.
With his gnarled hand
he honed an old trombone
in backyard bars and basement lairs
where music vibrated heat
harmonics couldn't contain.
Henry Bad Hand slid and jammed
Uptown, Downtown
and the wonder never left him.

Bolden

Dance hall fans beat lazy rhythms
in the heart of New Orleans.
Kid Bolden raised his cornet above the band's vanilla voice
and caught the throb of the crowd.
He'd taught himself the street songs,
the guitar pickers' blues,
the soul-bled rituals of the Baptist church
he could see from his living room.
It pushed out —
a working man's challenge to buttoned-down Creole bands.
In every Storyville cabaret
he played his heartbreak blues
until the music ate him.

Bolden's barber shop still stands
at the corner of First and Liberty -
two old chairs stare at the rusty mirror
into faded photographs.
Myth is king and color -
was it the women and whisky killed him
or, as Jelly Roll said,
He blew his brains out through his horn.

Swamped

Shadows shiver New Orleans March.
You feel Bienville's convict corps
as they try to rape the swamp.

Beneath Saint Louis Cathedral,
the ashes of an earlier church
expunge mixed blood parish records.

In Saint Louis Cemetery number one,
tombs perch above the sucking ooze that says
the river owns this delta and can reclaim it.

Cypress shadows mold malaria to mosquitoes;
ankle bells and antiphonal spells
hum you into dreamtime.

Rampart Street is four lanes now,
Congo Square a bench on the Vieux Carre
but New Orleans sunsets still breathe the swamp.

Italienische Reise

Der Mondstrahl is das Ruder,
Seerose dient als Boot;
Drauf fährt Pierrot den Süden
Mit gutem Reisewind.

— Schoenberg, Pierrot Lunaire, II.20

The moonbeam is his rudder,
waterlily serves as boat;
Pierrot sails southward
driven by good wind.

(translation, the author)

Centers

From the circled centers, power pulsed.
Ley lines spidered the continuum of crust.
Standing stones, earth mounds, dolmens
moved in testaments
of faiths lost to the common tongue.
Henges were mauled
in some frenzy to snuff the candles dark,
yet the stones still stand —
each unique in its orchestration
whispers from the fog dreamed wind
and tingles as you touch it.

Tongues

Older than Stonehenge,
Saracen stones stand at Avebury,
shrouded with why and when the Serpent
coiled the solar slide
wind and mist align in dark stones mortared -
pagan and Christian twined,
earth god to saint,
fires to candles lit inside the spired vaults,
fire and candle spilled
to sever the circle's power.

On foggy days, the moors still tingle;
barrows and ley lines cross the earth serpent
and Avebury stones still arch
for rain to loose their tongues.

Talking Back

Stones surround a sacred silence
where the old gods stare
at unrelenting night.
Ancient causeways overgrow
with trees and mustard grass.
I pass beyond the first circle;
run my hands along hard land
and pray in symbols no one hears.

We welcome danger when the moon spills
for we believe each wounding
spells another layer
talking at the dark
and silent runes breed shadows
worn like silver sickles;
earth robe folded dolmens
circle   full circle talking back at dark.

Trewyn Studio

Full of air waiting for magic
of Cornish stone made live
by forge and mallet,
Men-an-tol born and reborne,
Bronze Age thought transformed
when gods and winds were the only sculptors
and hands of man ran bright with blood.

What *Creative* forced their presence in this place,
walls aloud with white washed hills
and bells that tolled from granite towers
or churches centuries old?

Cornish rocks breathed before their folds knew much
about stone spirits
or messages of gods.

Trewyn Garden

Sculpted in the hillside,
stones laid stepwise and erect -
sea forms marble frozen,
monolithic bronzes holed to see
the tree leaves dance, feel the bell tones
form paths to a distant Celtic magic
that silences the birds.

Ponded gardens, forms in forms
turned, turned out, turned inside out
and frozen forms that carve man's space
in the green and blossom blood red
wind curves and lines to trunk, to sun,
to stuccoed walls and cobbled granite,
to the slate rooftops of Saint Ives,
to the bell and birdsong chorus
until stone bronze quicken with light.

Invasion

Old soldier eyes touch
tombstones white in the fog
they remember the firestorms,
the bodies; flat mounds
under fireflies strafing
fox holes and tanks;
the landscape of arm bands
blacker than death dreams
fly screaming wings pointed silver
resistance
of hay maws, grain fields and barns
utter empty,
the rain rusted
bonfires bandaged in blood
for the white crossed
pierres Normandes.

Normandy Beach

April swells with willow rain,
flattens leaves along maple stems,
froths light with the sweat gleam of frog.

Rain rubbed a slate roof
in Normandy,
walls foot thick granite
sills that stilled the patter soft call
of thrushes and horn owls
rubbed loose by our two lip glance.

Rain bows the blue haze forget me not;
rain pours libations to swallows
ablaze with their tender plain song.

Rain ringed the scrollwork
arcs pointed diamond down
rain drummed all
the meadows dissolved
in a testament
to blossom and leaf fold.

Rain dimmed the starburst
of the Sainte Chapelle
I followed you through the rosary
of blood genuflections.

Tones hard edged as stone
sing the rain raw mornings
you call me
but the river flows past a remembrance
of mallards
in the sun flash of green.

Vie en Rose

Inhale the fragrance
of cafe au lait;
listen to the
clink of saucers
in the courtyard
where roses sun
in the shadow
of the swastika.

Lascaux

Wizard beast, your lancet horns
herd the bulls and woolly ponies;
ponies race the dew dawn,
ponies and bulls rush;
stags splash
their head tossed horns
and bison bent back to back.
The tunnels spiral
the mother line.
Eye green growls light hunger
the deep ken voices ride;
torches lick ochre the blood rock
deep in caves
in our skulls double twisted,
deep in the last dark drop
to bison thrall,
a bird man writhes.

Pamplona

Caught on the hubris of horns,
the blood butterfly,
a ruby bath rains on voices
raised to the sky sword;
hooves pound dirt smoke,
the blood spore
young muscles pulse
the sweat flow of flesh
bellows resurrected
to circle the horns,
the heat stroke,
gray veils of crow breath
rattle the bead bones
crossing the sun.

Mordida

Manolete dances the skulls
his ballet whirls a cape
horns rape sideways;
the wind bows
his cape,
the rage of bull tongues
screaming the blood death.
Muscles and hooves tap the dust
whirlwind he laughs,
the collective.
Breath crosses eye orbs,
holes in hands,
the flash flesh,
red piss and bull sweat,
eyes white in the circle
hooves paw
bone fingers twirling a cape
horns rake and toss -
El/Asherah, Shiva-Nandi,
his hands raise invincible
steps hollow the blood road.
Horns impale the sky.

Whitewash

My view of Toledo
under Greco's throbbing sky
floats crystal prisms
whitewashed by sun
and shadow flowers run
against the somber hills.
I feel the anguished spirits
of peasants overrun
and twisting machinations
of governments become
god grown hierarchies
too heavy
to bear the burden
of their obsession with death.

No Exit

Tail worn wand,
I wing the claret sunset.
Ragegrief burns my brooding tongue;
goblets chime blood,
harmonicas and psychophones
stave dead men's haunts -
Zug, Fuss Zug,
Heidelberg, Zurich, Werfen, Mont Blanc;
my boots lace loaves of Bauernbrot,
raclette viande seche;
clouds lock down the Gletscherschlucht;
milk foams Berliner, croissant, baguette,
I am lost.

What might forests have done to me
had the city not encroached?
I wander the hostel crunch,
cold air shower Einzelzimmer,
toilet down the hall,
featherbeds patched and ironed,
breakfast with dog tail wagging
two thousand miles —
home calls me.
I cannot.

In green glass crevasses,
forest black as stick broomed earth,
my verbs lie in a tangle
more potent than my heart.

The train watches
rock me through the click click
of steel wheels;
ferry boat sails fill
the Bodensee.
My hair blows
among the Roman ghosts.
In Koblenz, my passport
is canceled by crows.

In Heidelberg

the birds first talked to me
when gray lit the tree tangled sky;
an alchemy of bird tongues ghosted the garret
and I was in a world of feather nuance
and willow piped surround.

Stone bridges arched the Nekar
as it trolled to the Rhine.
Street cobbles, buildings filled
with the books of centuries
but nowhere were the avian scores.

The castle ruins on the hill
felt more castle for its broken sills
and the lightning struck twice
tingled chambers
talons scratched in the walls.

Here, I realized Riesling's plainsong,
here I found Haydn in sidewalk tables
chickadees conducted,
here I sipped the lark song
that haunted Respighi's chords.

Turning Circles

I chop at the grass grown to hay,
fork it in windrows
for the sun to suck up its juice
and I think of the Austrian hillsides
patchworked with daisies and pinto cows
and the farmer who asked me to marry him.

He held my hands tightly,
hands of a milkmaid, he said
as he kissed each finger down.
I saw myself in the woman at the hostel,
back bent from forking
hillsides too steep for plows.
His sorrow a knife edge,
his limp a reminder of the wife lost,
his hands feather soft on my breast,
his tongue on my tongue
the slurred Werfen dialect
slow waltz and chablis.

The woman at the hostel thought me crazy
to deny the towns' wealthy widower -
she said the free village women all wanted him,
but I had sucked in the wild mistral -
I had to catch the train.

My scythe swings the moist green air.
Golden heads drop sun waterfall
to the laughter of creek.
Black and white sheep ring the pasture
where red hens dance on leg stems.
By hand I turn my garden rows,
by hand I turn the hay -
hands of soil roughened fingers
content at last to farm.

Wiener Blick

The train dead stopped on the track to Wien.
Tod. Ein Kind, we hear
but not what a child is doing on the rails.
Polizei parents ambulance
we stare at the blistering somewhere beyond
steel wheels the land curves the Wienerwald.

The train tunnels into our spy assignation,
the station shadow vaults well.
Mozart and four Strausses waltz Danube filigree —
Schönbrunn, Hofbrau, Zwiebeltürme,
crystal chandelier candles shining mirrors watching
golden Engeln Kachelofen glazed;
die Ringstrasse circles century-filled moat;
schöne Brunner singen Niebelungenlieder.

The streets stretch buildings balanced to toe
sidewalks, Wienertorte Kaffee mit Schlag;
music spills from practice halls
and grandes salles and the opera house blazes white marble.

A twice walk around half-block Esterhazy Park,
suitcase wheels bump for the blind alley
rumpled room courtyards zum goldenes Lamm.

Zauberflöte swell the cobbled boot tread
and always the Lippizaner white manes waving hoof high
ghosts in the Schloss-theater Marie Antoinette danced
as a shepherdess.

Above Montreux

grapes ripen flower fields.
Lac Leman clear as Byron's hand
ripples riffs of Coltrane.
From l'église de Glion you see
the Dents du Midi and Chillon
where Mademoiselle de Bonnivard lived with rats.

The viol beats her heart
strings saxophone eyes,
cafes on the promenade,
sails and blue skies -
the mountains rise sans vallonnements
to block the cold north winds.
A trumpet syncopates the beat
of Friday markets en plein air -
she was chained there,
watched her brothers die,
heard the lake face gray.

White foams the wake of skiers now;
the Geneva ferry glides;
the clear air rides on wings of Monk.
Church bells call us to prayer.
Glaciers wind the drum
rolls bet on black
crow notes against sun clef.

In Zurich

the hostel is run by nuns -
small cells, hard beds,
ten o'clock curfew,
coffee black, crusted buns.
The man mowing lawns
sings Aida.
Birds twine the waterpath,
every block a bank
spikes mountain spires.
Gruss Gott, they say to strangers.
Porches plait geranium showers,
rose cheeked children in gardens;
rose bells toll matins.
Dawn walks the lake path
blue jay canary cardinal
chocolate eyes three languages,
k's hard as brass
beams handrail polished
granite floors.
Edelweiss cows chew a guilded Angelus
to shine the glacier clouds.
Gold is the passport we watch
diamonds ice the shops;
bank on meadows full of buttercups.

Unter den Linden

Leaves wallow in sun wind,
air charged electric with pre-frost
tosses golden
hearth shadows in the flame thrust.
We worry life passing
too fast our thickening pulse
measures the day years -
seeds to saplings to trunks
slough rose petal parchments
scrolled in our first frenzied love
like leaves fly to ground
all the minutes we wasted
when summer lay lazy
and land spilled its seed.

Aprés le Deluge

Under the beak of the Weimar eagle
Berlin lies, still city of birds.
Peacocks, mallards, Himalayan Doves,
nightingales, magpies, yellow-beaked grebes
at the crossroads,
the mud milling gardens and forests
welcome the feathers, the fluttering whispers
of a city rising from ashes.
The ancient rubble wall long ago used
to renew the moveable feasts
to the wind the four chargers
tore from the Brandenburg Gate
with the fates of the people in bands
on their shoulders, bands on their arms;
the eagles screamed for blood.
No Three Penny Opera, the music reminds
of the rattle of bullets and bombs
but now that the union has come,
duck calls and swan songs
shower the city with birds.

Dubrovnik

A Dresden doll sits beside an old man's crooked arm.
You note he wears gloves and coat
and then you see the rough torn stones;
the window that is no window
but a wall broken free
and the tattered rags upon his bed
are cast with plaster wounds.

Slowly the sound of smoke drifts in,
the screams and moans of people mangled;
the red tile roofs are pools of blood
beneath the ashen stone.
Sweet-tongued larks sing along
with the blast of homemade bombs
as a city that nurtured Mongols and Turks
before the last oppressors spawned
blows itself to Hell.

We grieve for what cannot be —
the idyll of brotherhood;
the squeak of ancient wheels,
the solid bells that toll a time for prayer.
The waters of the Adriatic
wash timeless against salt sores
while a broken sky
sighs at the firework stars.

Schrei

Mere miles from the Virgin shrine
at Medjugorje, a trinity of camps
detain new Musselmänner
thin as any not fed by the SS —
brown faces rock carved
in the heart of bone dark eyes hollow
scores without water or
barbed screams ringing shot-trodden earth;
lines thrown hopeless
at stone soup.

On the Road to Peshawar

Khatack farmers gild the wind,
beat and toss stalks the way their fathers
gnawed centuries from the steep deep
wells their children's eyes
seed bread baked gold as the ribbon road
winding Bannu to Peshawar,
gold as the clear air dream dance
sabers swish the slow drummed
earth teeth tearing cloud.
Heads bow and wrap the drum bark
foot sandal to wind
paves an ancient trail to Peshawar.
Bright flowerbird lorries
grind the hot packed dust
winds the white tipped spine of the world,
the Kyber Pass mouth of the silk route to China.
Peshawar Herodotus called Kaspaturos.
Peshawar city still after old Taxila and Charsadda
lie dusty mounded bones.
Peshawar city Islamic since Mahmud of Chazri
though the Raj left its broad cantonment
by narrow street bazaars.
The Ossa Khawani, street of story tellers, story-less now,
the massive walls of Babur's Bohalisar
draw you through the needle eye -
kebabs, unleavened bread, tobacco and cardamom,
burkas and bangles; trays and samovars.
Cars and horse cabs muscle tourists
vendors call in Pashti, Farsi, Urdu, English; Punjabi
along the old silk road to China; the newold whirling commerce
that spells out Peshawar.

Leap of Faith

Glass beads, sharp as nails in my palm,
reflect the shards of sun -
rainbow shards, ghost edged
in the stained half light of the golden dome.
These beads, blessed by St. Peter's passed down hand,
numb my stumbling lips.
My eyes rove the shadow coves
candles flicker but the soul tongues
do not speak
only Michelangelo's ivory icons
polish the loss long carved out.
I feel the belly of this beast rumble,
feel its tail sift gold.
The tour moves en masse to the tapestries,
jewels, paintings, the Sistine Chapel.
God's arm is full of scratches,
his beard swirls me into smoke   I am damned
in the rush of wings   virile angels,
Adam's lush torso.

Outside the Vatican

black-veiled madonnas pass,
their hands folded, their baskets
like babies on their arms.
A gaggle of children hold out hands.
I answer their stories
in French or Spanish   they laugh,
follow me down the Via Santa Marcello,
la Via della Muratte
to where Agrippa's water *vergine* spews
Neptune drawn by two Tritons.
Two bambinos catch my coins to the fountain,
bless themselves in Trevi water,
and disappear.

The balconies are hung with washing,
with pots of herbs and blooms;
inside a church in no guide books,
the quiet embrace of nuns lighting candles,
the sweet incense of prayer.
In the corner, a priest hears confessions,
at the altar the chalice shines.
Brass candelabras hang suspended,
their crystal sparkling the cross.
Tears from Christ wash our feet -
the splinters rain heavy as thorns.

Maze

Taxis stall the tailspin turns
cabbies shout with their arms;
their voices din
the garlic rush of the Pizzeria
that bubbles above catacombs, Roman ruins;
the unrelenting marble kisses
and madonnas too remote
for hot oregano.

A haze embraces the hills today -
mazes of filtered shadows
wind the street backs.
Pigeon shades soften the blank-eyed
stare of the Coliseum
where blood binds the roots of stone lions.
Wind pipes the tunnels gladiators raced
to the arena;
the crowd roared   blood waters the grass.

The thousand year walls still draw spectators
though the battles are fought by ghosts —
rumor says Rome will fall with the Coliseum
and with it, the world.
The Arch of Constantine
marks the end of the Via Sacra
and the stone fountain
where contest survivors washed.

Saint Peter in Chains

There are crowds at the Vatican,
crowds in the museums,
but the church where Julius II rests
echoes my empty kneels.
The overload of nubile bodies
sends me back and back to the Moses —
his work rolled shoulders,
the ropy veins in his arms,
his big hands restless as they pose,
his beard twisted with the rage of vows.
His frown sears the scars on our souls.
The tablet wears him down
to the sheen of old leather
draped on his lap.
I listen for the clink of anvils,
wait for candles
to ignite his bush.

Italienische Reise

Firenze, the wheels shout, *Firenze*
all the way from Rome.
The conductor tells me
butterflies hover on grape wings
and olives coax secrets from cats.
Firenze is a city for lovers, he tells me,
a city of curves and thighs.

I meet him on the steps of the fort, Vincente,
a soldier on a pass.
We climb this fortress turned barracks
to art;
watch the mauve way light rolls the Tuscan hills,
lick Italian ice at a sidewalk table,
our lips blushing sunshine
we walk.

Hand in hand we stroll the Ponte Vecchio
where goldsmiths set up their shops
hanging out over the Arno,
the Arno flows under the Holy Trinity
rebuilt with stones from the first
bombs bowed her shoulders   my soldier
leans over the Arno and smiles.

Arm in arm we seek
the slow feast of eyes in the piazzas,
Cellini's Perseus,
David in the clear noonday sun,
his face determined, troubled,
his young man's body
marble cool to the touch —
Michelangelo's silken polish
is soft as a lover's throat.

We stand in the Santa Croce Basilica,
take in its white arched brows,
its rustic Franciscan trussing,
Giotto's Coronation of the Virgin.
The prism of la Cappella Maggiore
dances in Vincente's eyes.

The Santa Maria del Fiore
is a study in subtle marbles
under Brunelleschi's nipple cupola;
in this Pietá, Nicodemus stands behind Christ
and Mary Magdalena before Mary.
Giotto's tall Campanile
banded by panels of man's slow ascent
wafts a musky perfume.

The Baptistery's cupola steeps Byzantine mosaics -
angel hierarchies, Genesis, Christ,
Christ judging us.
Dante breathes at the ghost of the font
dripping holy water to those he will damn.
The Ghiberti east door is a masterpiece,
ten panels from the Old Testament
guilt in bronze.
We kiss there and walk on.

The Porcellino, Taca's Bronze Boar
guards the Straw Market
where the Florentine artisans sell —
the women all look like Maria
before she gave up her son.
There are a dozen varieties of garlic,
grapes with the sweat of the earth,
cheese you could sculpt with a butter knife,
cheese sharp as teeth in the moonlight,
cheese that melts when we touch.

JO NELSON

teaches creative writing at Tacoma Community College, Gig Harbor and for writers' conferences. She has been a writer in residence for the Washington State Arts Commission, and has taught German, French, and English in Maryland and Colorado. Her poems, articles, and short stories have been published in numerous national anthologies and magazines including Blueline, Chachalaca, the Chariton Review, Confluence, Comstock Review, Dream Network, Frontiers, Harrisburg Review, the Horsethief's Journal, Lucid Stone, Main Street Rag, Natural Bridge, Out of Season, Pacific Coast Journal, Plainsongs, Pleiades, Portland Review, Poetry Seattle, Switched on Gutenberg, West Wing Review, and Willow Creek Journal. She is one of six poets in the anthology Seattle Five Plus One (Pig Iron Press) Her poem Tuning the Interior was used in an original composition for German radio by Johannes Schmidt-Sistermanns.

She reads by herself, with the Seattle Five Plus One, and with the Daughters of Dementia.

When she is not writing, Nelson works on her fixer farm and farmhouse that still look a bit like the Egg and I but are slowly moving toward being Beatrix Potter's place. She has goats, sheep, chickens, Muscovy ducks, a dog, and a pride of cats; grows flowers, vegetables and fruits, and is in the process of reforesting the part of her property that was clear cut years ago.